The reasons I chose to study where I did is:

What I was most nervous about before I left for my trip was:

I was looking most forward to:

My first 24 hours after I arrived went like:

My first week went like:

My first impression of my abroad location:

My living space can be described how

_____

_____

_____

_____

_____

_____

_____

_____

_____

_____

_____

_____

_____

_____

_____

_____

_____

_____

_____

_____

: What I can see from my windows:

From my living space, I can hear:

Walking down the street I typically see/hear:

The best way I found to combat homesickness:

I kept in touch with my family by:

Favorite food I found that I could eat all the time:

My favorite place that I found to eat out:

The best place to find a sweet treat:

The biggest physical challenges I faced:

The biggest emotional challenges I faced:

Funny Cultural misunderstanding/miscommunication I experienced:

My favorite thing to cook abroad:

My favorite memory is:

The places I visited include:

Where I want to visit again:

A typical weekend abroad was spent doing:

The weather was usually:

The locals enjoyed doing:

I felt like a local when I:

How I changed my behavior from a tourist to local:

How I usually got around the city/town/area:

Describe a time where you were proud of yourself:

Describe the friends you made on your trip:

I was surprised to see the locals doing:

The laundry situation included:

Shopping and Grocery stores were like:

Favorite place to hang out in my town was:

The best bar was:

A typical morning includes:

A typical evening includes:

Interesting people I met on my journey:

Friends I met along the way:

Where I would go to relax:

My classes were:

My favorite class was:

My abroad University is different from my University at home in what ways?:

My least favorite experience:

Skills and lessons I have learned from another culture include:

Differences between school at home and school abroad:

Cultural differences from home that I have noticed:

Someone I was influenced by and what they had to say:

How my experiences differentiated from my
expectations:

What I learned about traveling in general:

Local/healthy habits I picked up in my host country:

Advice I would give to someone preparing or considering studying abroad:

Upon returning home, how am I experiencing "reverse culture shock"?:

What I miss about my host country the most:

I learned about myself:

Memories:

Memories:

Memories:

Memories:

Memories:

Memories:

Memories:

Memories:

Memories:

Memories:

Memories:

Memories:

Memories:

Memories:

Memories:

Memories:

Memories:

Memories:

Memories:

Memories:

Memories:

Memories:

Memories:

Memories:

Memories:

Memories:

Memories:

Memories:

Memories:

Memories:

Memories:

Tickets / Memorabilia:

Tickets / Memorabilia:

Tickets / Memorabilia:

Tickets / Memorabilia:

Tickets / Memorabilia:

Tickets / Memorabilia:

Notes:

Notes:

Notes:

Notes:

Notes:

Notes:

Notes:

Notes:

Travel/Flight info:

Travel/Flight info:

Travel/Flight info:

Travel/Flight info:

Travel/Flight info:

Travel/Flight info:

Travel bucket list:

_____

_____

_____

_____

_____

_____

_____

_____

_____

_____

_____

_____

_____

_____

_____

_____

_____

_____

_____

_____

_____

_____

Travel bucket list:

Travel bucket list:

Travel bucket list:

Made in the USA
Columbia, SC
16 June 2022

61807416R00061